YOUR KNOWLEDGE HAS VALUE

Women in the Ottoman Empire. Elizabeth Craven

How are European cities presented in Elizabeth Craven's travelogues and to what extent do they differ from the representation of Russia?

Daniel Reiser

Bibliographic information published by the German National Library:

The German National Library lists this publication in the National Bibliography; detailed bibliographic data are available on the Internet at http://dnb.dnb.de.

ISBN: 9783389052389
This book is also available as an ebook.

© GRIN Publishing GmbH
Trappentreustraße 1
80339 München

Print and binding: Books on Demand GmbH, Norderstedt, Germany
Printed on acid-free paper from responsible sources.

GRIN web shop: https://www.grin.com/document/1493293

Universität Konstanz

FB Literaturwissenschaft

Winters Semester 2021/22

18th Century Orients: British Women Travellers in the Ottoman Empire

Introduction to Literary Texts

Elizabeth Craven's series of letters

"A journey through the Crimea to Constantinople"

How are European cities presented in Elizabeth Craven's travelogues and to what extent do they differ from the representation of Russia?

Daniel Reiser

Table of contents

1. Introduction

Elizabeth Craven is "a lesser-known writer was Elizabeth Craven, margravine of Anspach, whose *Journey through the Crimea to Constantinople* (1789) was addressed to a fictitious male friend" (Nussbaum, 137).

Elizabeth Craven (1750-1828) is known for a diverse life that was comprised of travelling, several love-affairs as well as scandals (see Gasper 12-31). She was born into the upper class of Georgian England and she became a celebrity (see Ibid.). Furthermore, she had six children in total (see Ibid.). Even though she faced a lack of education, since she was a woman and it was quite difficult for women to receive a proper education at this time, she managed to become famous through poetry writing, stories as well as plays (see Ibid.). She had to move to France after her marriage where she was living in seclusion (see Ibid.). She was travelling surprisingly all over Europe and created a series of letters that were addressed to a fictitious man (see Ibid.). These letters are one of her best-known works (see Ibid.). Furthermore, she was living in Germany as the companion and second of wife of the Margrave of Anspach (see Ibid.). In 1792, she and the Margrave settled in England (see Ibid). When she became older, she moved to Italy where she was mostly sailing, gardening and writing (see Ibid.). Even in her last years, Craven focused on her feminist principles and criticisms for which she was well known (see Ibid.).

Selected letters from Elizabeth Craven's series of letters which deal with her journey to Constantinople will be analyzed throughout this term paper. The focus of the paper is the outward journey to the Ottoman Empire and the return journey. Special attention is paid to how certain cities or countries in general are being presented by Craven, also focusing on the values of the individual cities and countries. The cities of Vienna and Athens are examined more closely and then Russia, or more precisely Petersburg, will be compared to the cities analyzed before.

The research question of this term paper is how the European cities are presented in Elizabeth Craven's travelogues and to what extent they differ from the representation of Russia. Throughout the analysis, the question of whether there is a collective of the West is also being pursued. After an analysis of the depiction of Vienna and Craven's experiences there, there will be a comparison with the experiences she made in Athens. The last step of the main part is to compare Vienna and Athens to Petersburg, respectively Russia in general. A final conclusion takes up all the important findings of this work.

Regarding the current state of research on Elizabeth Craven, it must be mentioned that there is not much literature on the series of letters which deal with her long journey through Europe to

Constantinople or – more precisely – with the individual cities in detail. The majority of the literature deals specifically with the Ottoman Empire itself and with the situations women had to face back then. Nevertheless, some interesting secondary literature could be researched. Among other things, the texts "Torrid zones" by Felicity A. Nussbaum that deals with women focusing on maternity and sexuality as well as a work about Craven and her travelogues by Julia Gasper who wrote about Craven as a writer, feminist and European could be included. The most interesting piece of work was Efterpi Mitsi's text on Craven's letters from Athens focusing on the female picturesque.

2. Analysis of Vienna

At the beginning of her journey to Constantinople, Elizabeth Craven visited Vienna. In the following, it will be examine how Craven describes the city of Vienna, its people as well as the local government.

Overall, she has a generally positive view on the city, as evidenced by her being impressed with its structure, particularly "the […] houses with comfortable chimnies" (Craven 162). A quite striking statement of Craven is when she says: "I must say that I never saw such a profusion of things" (Ibid. 168). That shows us that Craven initially did not expect Vienna to be so beautiful and that she is very surprised. Craven parallels her native England, as evidenced by her enthusiasm, for the great assemblies she finds both in London and Vienna (see Ibid. 170). Furthermore, Craven is fascinated by the city park in Vienna which is known as the "Prater" (see Ibid. 171). It is a park that is surrounded by many trees and the river Danube. She compares the "Prater" to an English park (see Ibid.), showing that she finds another parallel to her homeland. She is also particularly attracted to the zoological garden created by the Emperor.

A charming city always needs residents. Craven finds the Viennese ladies to be good-looking, educated and very polite (see Ibid. 164). Some of the women not only speak various foreign languages, but also read, write and speak good English (see Ibid. 163). Csendes and Opll recorded that the Viennese court was regarded as a humanistic center and that Latin was he language of the educated class (see Csendes & Opll 423). This shows that there were many intellectual people in Vienna and they made the cityscape appear positive. Furthermore, Craven notes during her stay in Vienna that the inhabitants are very musical and that she is sure that a young Englishman with a good education could spend his time every evening with ladies from the upper class (see Craven 163). At this point, this statement of Csendes and Opll is significant: "Die Kirchen der Stadt waren bemüht, ihre großen Feiern musikalisch würdevoll zu gestalten" (Csendes & Opll 525). Here it becomes clear that music is an integral part of Vienna. The ladies are furthermore described by Craven a "tall and faire – more handsome than pretty" (Craven 164). In addition, the people of Vienna are pictured as "generally fair" (Ibid. 169-170). It is quite striking that Craven even says that she could imagine spending her life with some of the Viennese ladies, since [t]hey have not the cold silent reserve of English women, nor the impertinent intéret for me, of the French ladies" (Ibid. 170).

Craven's stay is not only characterized positively, since she also has negative experiences in Vienna, but these are not the majority of her travelogue. Craven is generally positively impressed by Vienna. Still however she faced some negative situations. One of them is when she finds it suspicious that the women wear white make-up and that even girls around the age of 10 walk around the street with make-up which Craven thinks is rather incomprehensible (see Ibid. 169). Various political points can also be noted within Craven's travelogue. However, it is important to mention that Vienna is depicted as "die politisch zentrale und kulturell dominierende Stadt" (Csendes & Oppl 13). This shows that Vienna was generally very powerful and is considered accordingly in the context of the other cities that will be compared in the course of this work.

The conceptions of the Emperor in Vienna differ greatly from those of the King of England (see Craven 164). The Emperor, according to Craven, has parallels with the Queen of France, as Craven notes (see Ibid. 167), but the Emperor speaks very pleasantly and amusingly. According to Csendes and Oppl, the city of Vienna cannot be compared with any other major city in Europe (Csendes & Oppl 13) which – again – emphasizes its power. In addition, Vienna is to be regarded as an important economic and political partner for other countries. In her letters about Vienna, Craven mentions officer's dresses which she saw when she had an audience with the Emperor (see Craven, 165). From Craven's point of view, the Polish and Hungarian dresses in particular are very pretty. She mentions that each nation should keep their own individual dresses and style, since that is what defines a country (see Ibid.). Of particular note is the Prime Minister who described as a patriot and is portrayed as being very skilled. His franknesss and openness always accompany him because the well-being of the people is very important to him (see Ibid. 167-168).

In the end, Craven came to the conclusion in her letters about Vienna that she never experienced such a great place she wanted to visit together with her son.

3. Analysis of Athens

The next city to be examined is Athens. As the first female writer, Elizabeth Craven made her way to Athens (see Mitsi 19). It is important to mention that she questions well-known oriental representations throughout her journey to Greece (see Ibid.), sometimes even criticizes or rejects them. This will be examined in more detail in the course of the analysis of Athens.

In Greece, Craven experiences a severe storm on sea which results in her stranding on the island of Marmora. She is impressed by the bare rocks that rise out of the sea and by the rocks that have disappeared due to volcanic activity or the ones that have been rocked by earthquakes (see Craven 370-371). A visit to a grotto, which arouses her curiosity and fascinates her a lot, is very prominent in her travelogue (see Ibid. 365). Mitsi describes the grotto as "an emblem of beauty beyond history and culture" (Mitsi 29). The colors and shapes inspire Craven very much, so she says: "Nothing can be more beautiful than the shapes the chrystalisations have taken in some parts of the ceiling […] of this place" (Craven 365). This splendor of the fossils, the darkness of the grotto as well as the illuminations reflecting the site show the strangest and most beautiful landscape one can imagine (see Ibid. 368). A first parallel to Vienne can be drawn here, since Craven is also – as during her stay in Vienna – fascinated by the Greek landscape and the city of Athens. While in Vienna it is more about striking buildings, in Greece Craven is more attracted to the natural, for example the grotto. It is very significant to mention at this point that Craven was the first woman to enter this grotto (see Ibid. 367). The people who are with her designate her as a "supernatural being" (Ibid.). This action requires a lot of courage, as Mitsi describes in her text: "Craven's goal is not only to revisit […] places [that were] completely inaccessible to the male travellers to the Orient[,] but also to travel to the sites Montagu did not visit, to the islands of Greece and especially to Athens" (Mitsi 22). Furthermore, the direct experience is in the foreground (see Ibid. 21). Craven sometimes reaches her limits, which becomes clear when she states: "the smoke of the torches […] almost took my breath away, and I was forced to set myself down" (Craven 369). It is crucial to mention that "Craven's descriptions of spaces and places ignored by male travellers embodies a development in travel writing, determined not only by gender but also by the search for new sources of aesthetic pleasure" (Mitsi 24). It becomes clear that the focus is more on what people actually explore rather than who explores something, keeping in mind that it was quite difficult and dangerous for women back then to travel around the world like Craven did.

Overall, Craven describes the sights of Athens as rather positive. Among other things, she mentions the well-preserved temple called "Minerva", which is not damaged from the outside, but looks more like a ruin inside (see Craven 375). Here, too, she seems to be fascinated and in parts even overwhelmed, which can be analyzed in the following statement: "Nothing can exceed the magnitude of these enormous columns" (Ibid. 376).

Although this work does not explicitly deal with Ottoman Empire, Craven does discuss Turkish women in her travelogue. In the course of describing the magnificent temple, she mentions that this temple used to serve the Turks. She is rather condescending about the Turks, which becomes clear when she says that the Turks have no idea of the value of their treasures (see Ibid. 384). The Turks are described as ignorant, lazy, stupid and sluggish (see Ibid.). Mitsi's analysis comes to the conclusion that "Craven's concern about the fate of the antiquities is rather hypocritical, as it is not based on her admiration of ancient art" (Mitsi 28).

Craven stated that "the Athenians could neither form landscape or shade" (Craven 377-378), describing the art as a perfection (see Ibid.). Her statement that a small orange garden is more valuable that a large temple (see Ibid. 378) is quite striking. Mitsi figures that during the stay in Greece, Craven explores her preference for nature and scenic landscapes rather than made-made space (see Mitsi 28). This specifies the fact that Craven is highly fascinated by natural places such as this orange garden rather than by the temple she visited. Furthermore, she discovers groves, olive trees and another temple, the temple of Theseus (see Craven 371). Between the lines of her descriptions, an attitude with slightly negative connotations can be interpreted, since she begins her descriptions with "the only fine things which are seen" (Ibid.). This emphasizes the fact that the list of sites she experienced so far is not very long which furthermore implies a rather bored attitude.

Referring to the people of Athens, Craven describes Greek peasant women who suffer from different illnesses (see Ibid. 367). Compared to the poorer Greek women, Craven describes Turkish women as being rather well dressed and, depending on their men's positions, even appearing splendid (see Craven 373-374). Nonetheless, a negative attitude towards the Turks is also evident here, for she says: "[The Turks] who have really not the smallest idea of the value of treasures they possess, [...] destroy them wantonly on every occasion" (Ibid.). There is a very big contrast to Vienna, as – according to Craven – the Viennese women are educated, polite and good-looking (see Ibid. 164), whereas she pictures the Greek and especially the Turkish women as dark and sallow (see Mitsi 31-32). They are also vulgar and lazy (see Ibid.). Craven also finds the baths designed for women suffering from illnesses such as rheumatism and other diseases to be negative (see Ibid. 381-382). To Craven it is incomprehensible how women can expose themselves to such heat (see Ibid.). She describes Greek and Turkish women who sit there naked and then come out of the baths cooked (see Ibid.). These baths did not only serve the women for healing, but also for entertainment among themselves. Mitsi describes in this regard that women suffering from obesity have a repulsive effect (see Mitsi 31). Craven has never seen so many fat women at once, which leads her to speak of a disgusting spectacle (see Craven 382).

Finally, it should be mentioned that Elizabeth Craven was able to gain experience regarding music. In Vienna, she was positively impressed by the music. In Athens, on the other hand, Craven becomes a spectator of various dances which she describes as a "stupid performance"

(Ibid. 383). She describes the music as boring and sleepy, whereas the music in Vienna was rather described as positive and one could feel that Craven really enjoyed it there.

With regard to the initial question of this paper, focusing on the similarities and differences of the European cities (in comparison to Russia), it can be stated that Vienna and Athens do not have very much in common. Possible points of intersection can be found, for instance, in terms of the fascination by Craven when she discovers the city and landscape of both Vienna and Greece. Concerning the inhabitants, Vienna differs greatly from the Athenians, since from Craven's point of view the people, especially the women, in Vienna are friendly, good-looking and intelligent while the Athenians are rather described as vulgar, lazy, dark and sallow. It should be said that in Vienna Craven was more fascinated by buildings and music, while Athens stands out with numerous naturally created places.

In the context of the collective of the West, it can be said that Vienna and Athens have little in common, as shown by the analysis. In contrast to Vienna, oriental values are represented in Athens respectively Greece in general. From that it one can conclude that Greece differs from the Western values and this therefore interferes the formation of such a collective.

4. Analysis of Petersburg

After the analysis of the experiences in Vienna and Athens, the analysis of Petersburg is following. Craven claims that she finds the area between Warsaw and Petersburg quite boring and describes it as very flat (see Craven 183). Before a detailed analysis of Craven's experiences and description of Petersburg in context, it is important to mention that Petersburg was to be seen as the "window to Europe" (Gutsmiedl-Schümann et al. 576) and was describes as the "new capital of the empire and exemplary city of European layout" (Ibid.). To many English travellers who were heading to Russia, including, Elizabeth Craven, Russia appeared like a large raw diamond with a precious interior that still needs to be cut (see Anton 172). From this statement it can be concluded that Russia was seen as a country that had a certain degree of insecurity and distance towards Europeans respectively the European values. Still however, Petersburg has adapted to the European values in many different areas which is also shown by Craven.

Upon arriving in Petersburg, Craven states that "Petersburg is a cheerful and fine looking town; the streets are extremely wide and long" (Craven 187). Furthermore, "there are buildings erected for the reception of Arts and Science of every kind; for artists or amateurs […] to fix in the present capital of this vast empire" (Ibid.). Gutsmiedl-Schümann et al. state that "Saint Petersburg was designed as a city with regular plan, entirely uncharacteristic of Russian cities that had been built chaotically since the Middle Ages" (Gutsmiedl-Schümann et al. 576). Here, one can already see that Petersburg differs immensely from other Russian cities which makes Petersburg a unique city. It shows that Petersburg is stands out from other cities due to its different structure which is also described by Craven throughout her travelogue. Craven describes that the houses are decorated with the most magnificent furniture from all countries (see Craven 192). Helmut Anton says that Craven has doubts about these extraordinary buildings and is skeptical as to whether this culture can last (see Anton 184). Not only the city, but also the Russian way of life, especially that of the nobles, is very extravagant. Everyone wants to vie with one another with even more luxury and fashion (see Ibid. 187).

According to Craven, only the Empress and Princess wear typical Russian clothing. So Craven feels it a pity that nations do not keep their own fashions (see Ibid. 188). At first glance, the Empress with her black air and dark blue eyes as well as her dark skin color seems a bit arrogant to Craven (see Anton 193). Regarding the residents of Russia, Craven states: "I am assured the Russians are deceitful" (Craven 200). Craven writes that Russia would probably be a safe country if one could do without French luxury and English comfort (see Ibid. 189).

Nonetheless, Craven is surprised that the Russians hold English merchants in high esteem. In question of privilege, there are regular negotiations from government to government (see Anton 169) which shows that Russia is an important partner on the one hand and quite willing to compromise on the other. In contrast to Vienna and Athens, Craven also suspects that Russia is one of the cheapest countries to live in (see Craven 189). Concerning the upbringing of the youth, Craven clearly shows that she has doubts when she sees describes that she sees in the young people a mixture of pedantry and debauchery which can only degenerate into impertinence and folly (see Ibid. 190). In general, the citizen is convinced that only honesty can increase (see Ibid.).

Craven has positive experiences when the Empress visits. She meets some pretty, witty young Russian ladies who are very successful (see Ibid. 192). Compared to Vienna, various counts and dukes give equally magnificent balls here. Thus, in her letters, Craven also mentions the music which she describes as harmonic (see Ibid. 194). Here, she can draw comparisons to Vienna, since music played a concise role there, which, unfortunately, she had not found in

Athens in the same form. Furthermore, Craven is visits the Hermitage which will occupy a beautiful row of rooms after completion (see Ibid. 195). Thus, Craven notes that the Empress tries everything to bring the customs, science and comforts of other countries to Petersburg (see Ibid. 200).

In her letters about Petersburg, Craven contradicts the prejudice that the Russians are wrong when she says: "I am assured that the Russians are deceitful" (Ibid.), as mentioned earlier. What is striking is her statement that she does not want to part with the Russian ladies, because – according to Craven – they have many talents and she could not have imagined a better company, which is made clear by the following statement: "Wit and talents will always be objects of importance to me; I have found them here, and shall be sorry to quit them" (Ibid.). Just like in Vienna, the women in Petersburg know different languages and are open to other peoples which are positive traits, respectively talents (see Ibid.).

As the analysis of Petersburg has now shown, the three cities of Vienna, Athens and Petersburg are very different, although there are some similarities.

The most striking similarity is the magnificent houses and buildings that can be found in both Vienna and Petersburg. Craven is also positively impressed by the city park called Prater and in Petersburg by the various buildings for science and art. With regards to Athens, it can be said that the city does not adorn itself with magnificent buildings, but rather archaeological treasures.

Regarding to the inhabitants of the respective cities, it can be said that Craven portrays the Viennese women and Russian women quite positively. According to her, these women are educated, personable and well-dressed. In Athens, on the other hand, Craven meets women who are more interested in oriental culture. She describes them as fat and sluggish, being shocked of the fact that they share the bathrooms and appear in such a way.

As for the music, Craven is clearly more taken with Vienna as well as Petersburg, since she described the music in Athens as rather boring. In addition, magnificent balls are taking place in both Vienna and Petersburg which do not exist in this form in Athens at all.

In order to pursue the question of whether there is a Western collective, it must be said that this is a quite difficult question to answer. It must be however noted that, surprisingly, Vienna and Petersburg are more similar than Vienna and Athens for example. Since Petersburg has some European characteristics, including, for example, the imperial family which both Vienna and

Petersburg have, Petersburg and hence Russia does show more European roots than Athens does. This concerns at least the points discussed in the individual analysis of the three cities.

5. Conclusion

With this term paper, the three cities of Vienna, Athens and Petersburg should be analyzed in terms of structure, people, culture etc. and it should be looked at to what extent they differ, in particular how Vienna and Athens differ from Russia. In addition to that, the question of whether there is a Western collective, i. e. a collective based on European values, was investigated. However, this question was relatively difficult to answer, as the analysis of the tree cities mentioned above has shown.

Within the individual analyses, not only the structure of the respective cities was examined, but above all the inhabitants of the cities and the cultural area, for example music and dance. Regarding Vienna, the analysis of Elizabeth Craven's travelogue has shown that Vienna is generally portrayed relatively positively and Craven is very impressed by the structure of the city itself. Apart from the magnificent houses that fascinate her, she writes about a city park and river as well as, above all, about the importance of music in the city. Regarding the residents, she notes that they are very good looking, educated and polite. Craven mentions this positively and is impressed that the Viennese ladies have such good skills when it comes to foreign languages.

Concerning the next city to be examined, Athens, Craven is clearly sceptical about it and even questions oriental depictions there. She describes the landscape there as strange and at the same time very beautiful. In Greece, Craven is particularly impressed by the places created by nature. For instance, she visits a grotto which is she is very fond of. Overall, she is not overly overwhelmed by the breadth of places she visits. In comparison to Vienna, she is clearly not as positive here, and the way her experiences are written down reveals a tendency towards a bored attitude. In the course of her letters about Athens, she also rants about Turkish women whom she presents as lazy and stupid. Craven is very shocked about the fact that such fat women can meet in baths for entertainment and in order to heal themselves.

The last city, Petersburg, is considered a window to Europe. With regard to Craven's experiences, it could be analyzed that she describes the city as cheerful and good-looking, even as unique if you consider Petersburg in the overall Russian context. She realizes that Petersburg differs greatly from the rest of Russia. Overall, however, she describes Russia as a generally safe country with a lot of power and says that she imagines life there to be very cheap. In addition to the imperial family, which also exists in Vienna for instance, Petersburg shines with its international connections to e. g. England. Furthermore, she finds the people to be friendly and intelligent, although she has a few doubts, for example concerning the education of younger people as well as the structure of the city with its magnificent furniture from all over the world.

In summary, for a more profound answer to the question of a Western collective, one would indeed have to consider and analyze more European cities, in order to be able to find a broader answer that builds on different perspectives. The cities analyzed in this term paper have shown that in terms of a collective of the West, Vienna and Petersburg tend to have a lot of parallels, while Athens is less likely to be classified as purely Western and hence it is difficult to say that Greece could be part of such a collective or not. With regards to further analyses, it would be exciting to include France or Italy, for example, in order to be able to go into more detail concerning the values of the West and to determine whether and how such a collective can be formed in the end.

6. Bibliography

Primary source:

Craven, Elizabeth. *A Journey through the Crimea to Constantinople*. The John Hopkins University Press, 1995.

Secondary sources:

Anton, Helmut. *Englische Russlandsreise im 18. Jahrhundert* in: *Jahrbücher für Geschichte Osteuropas*. Franz Steiner Verlag, 1936, pp. 169-200.

Gasper, Julia. *Elizabeth Craven: Writer, Feminist and European*. Vernon Press, 2017.

Gutsmiedl-Schümann, Doris et al. *Some insights into the lives of builders of early Saint Petersburg* in: Bertèmes, François et al. *Praehistorische Zeitschrift*, Band 95 Heft 2, p. 576-577.

Mitsi, Efterpi. *Lady Elizabeth Craven's Letters from Athens and the Female Picturesque* in: Kolocotroni, Vassiliki & Efterpi, Mitsi. *Women Writing Greece – Essays on Hellenism, Orientalism and Travel*. Editions Rodopi B. V., 2008, pp. 19-35.

Nussbaum, Felicity A. *Torrid Zones – Maternity, Sexuality, and Empire in Eighteenth-Century English Narratives*. The John Hopkins University Press, 1789.